A Little Book of Hours

FOR SOLO PIANO

Peter Sculthorpe

FABER *ff* MUSIC

© 1998 by Faber Music Ltd
First published in 1998 by Faber Music Ltd
3 Queen Square London WC1N 3AU
Cover design by S & M Tucker
Cover quotation: Annette Morreau
Music processed by Peter Sculthorpe and Christopher Hinkins
Printed in England by Halstan & Co Ltd

ISBN 0-571-51876-1

A Little Book of Hours was given its first performance by Jean Hasse
at the Deal Summer Music Festival, 6 August 1998.

To buy Faber Music publications or to find out about the full range of titles available
please contact your local retailer or Faber Music sales enquiries:
Tel: +44 (0)1279 82 89 82   Fax: +44 (0)1279 82 89 83
Email: sales@fabermusic.com   Website: www.fabermusic.com

PREFACE

A Book of Hours was originally a collection of prayers, each prayer, in Latin, to be recited at a certain time of the day. In the later Middle Ages, these books came to be illustrated in fanciful ways. The gilded decorations, now much-treasured, depict matters ranging from daily events to the cycle of life itself.

Inspired by this idea, *A Little Book of Hours* reflects some aspects of a day in the life of Koori children. The Koori people are Aborigines of south eastern Australia. In the music, the evening star heralds a lullaby; and the morning star heralds a song of sunrise; this is followed by dancing, which comes to an end as the sun gathers its strength. The six pieces are musically inter-related: some of the connections reveal themselves easily, and some are hidden, awaiting discovery.

Peter Sculthorpe, January 1998

VORWORT

Ein Stundenbuch war ursprünglich eine Sammlung von Gebeten in lateinischer Sprache, wobei jedes Gebet im Tagesverlauf zu einer bestimmten Zeit gesprochen werden mußte. Im späteren Mittelalter wurden diese Stundenbücher auf phantasievolle Weise ausgeschmückt. Die heute äußerst kostbaren vergoldeten Abbildungen zeigen Motive, die dem Alltagsleben entnommen sind, die aber auch den Kreislauf des Lebens selber widerspiegeln.

Angeregt durch dieses ursprüngliche Konzept des Stundenbuches, vermittelt *A Little Book of Hours* (Das kleine Stundenbuch) Einblick in einen Tag im Leben der Koori-Kinder. Das Aborigine-Volk der Koori lebt im Südosten Australiens. In der Musik von Sculthorpe wird das umgesetzt, indem der Abendstern ein Wiegenlied ankündigt, der Morgenstern dagegen ein Lied zum Sonnenaufgang. Es folgen dann verschiedene Tänze, die mit den letzten Sonnenstrahlen enden. Die sechs Stücke sind musikalisch miteinander verbunden; einige Zusammenhänge sind offensichtlich, andere dagegen sind versteckt und erschließen sich erst bei näherer Beschäftigung mit dem Werk.

Peter Sculthorpe, Januar 1998

Duration: *c.*6'30"

A Little Book of Hours

PETER SCULTHORPE

I. Evening Star

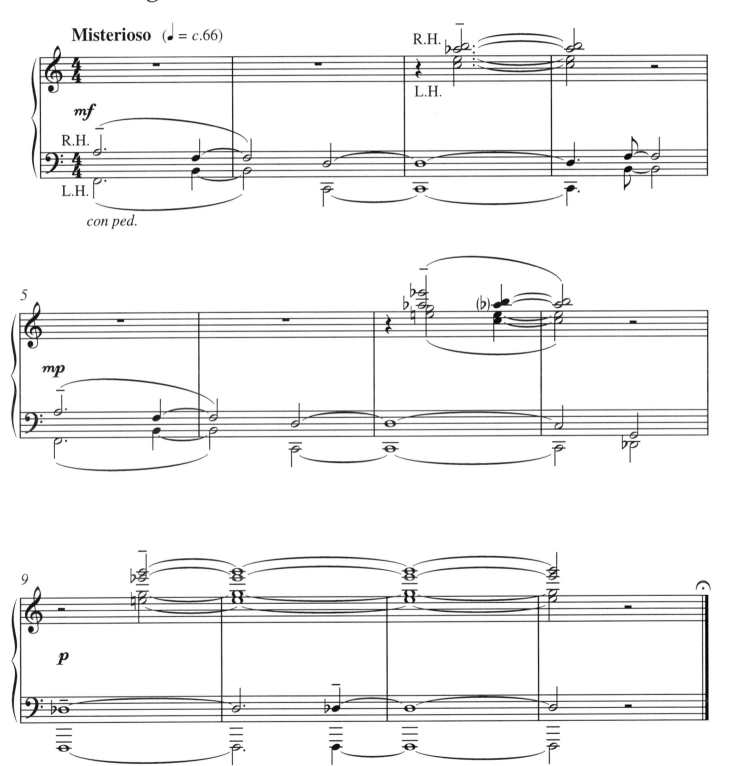

II. Koori Dreaming

III. Morning Star

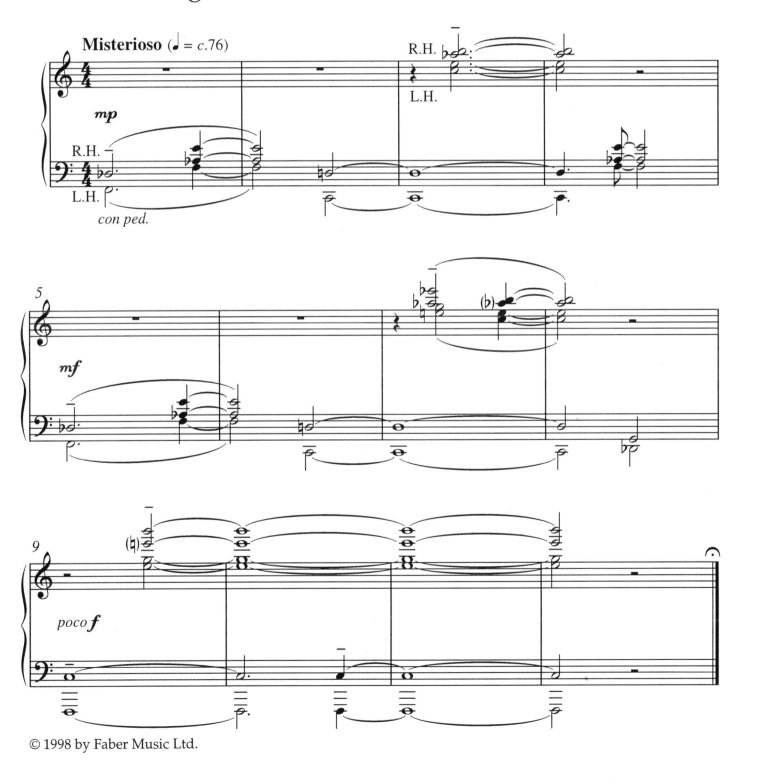

IV. Sun Singing

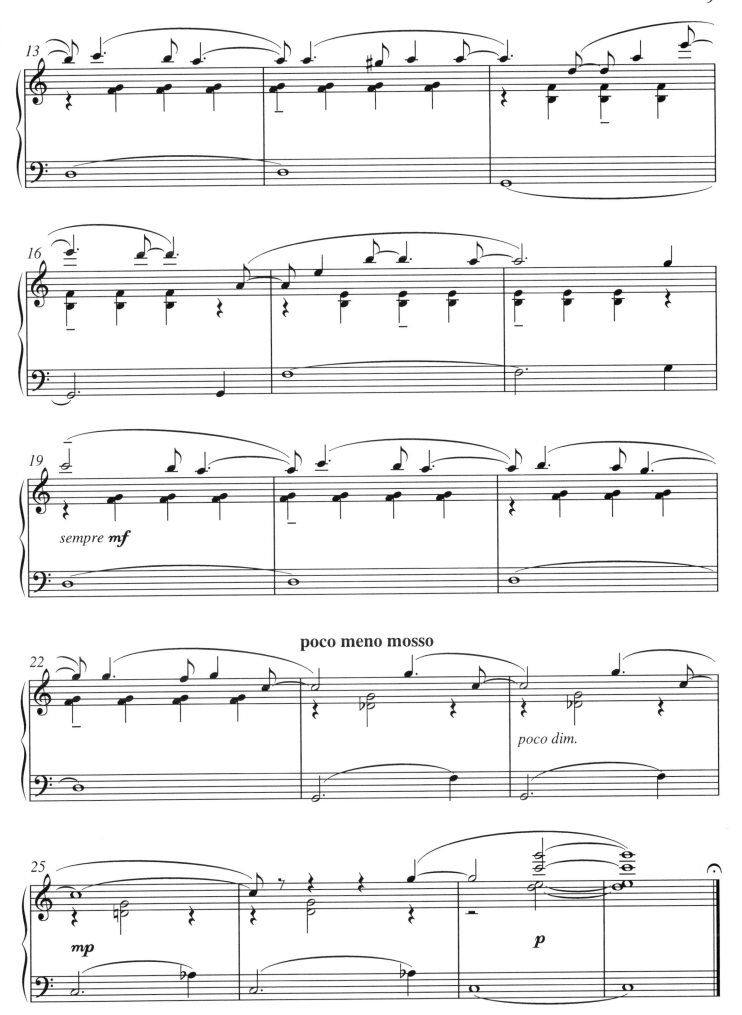

V. Koori Dancing

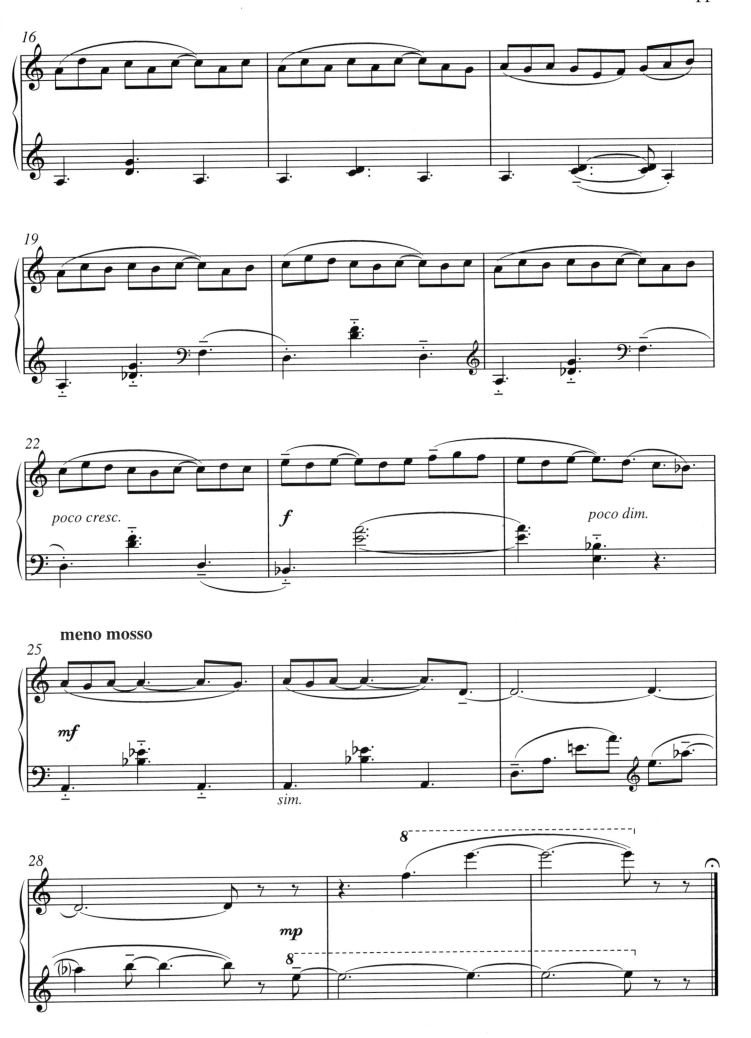

VI. Singing Sun

Sydney, January 1998